# Decoration

# Brightly lit spaces

*Decoration*

arco
editorial

**AUTHOR**

Francisco Asensio Cerver

**EDITOR IN CHIEF**

Paco Asensio

**PROJECT CO-ORDINATOR**

Ivan Bercedo (Architect)

**TRANSLATION & PROOF READING**

David Clough

**DESIGN & LAYOUT**

Mireia Casanovas Soley

**PHOTOGRAPHERS**

Richard Bryant/Arcaid, Mario Ciampi, Stephane Couturier/ Archipress,
Francesc Tur, Paolo Mussat, Joshio Shiratori, Lurdes Jansana, Reiner
Blunck, Lluís Casals, Wolfwang Hoyt/Esto, Michael Morán, Deidi Von
Schaewen, Peter AAraon, Emma Duval, Alan Weintraub, Carla de
Benedetti, Hennie Raaymakers, Friedhelm Thomas, Sérgio Antão, Scott
Francis-Esto, Eduard Hueber, Vincent Knapp, Peter Kopp, Thomas
Pritschert, Gary Rogers, Gert Von Bassewitz, Tito Dalmau, Ernst
Giselbrecht, Julie Philipps, Timothey Husley, Michael Photiadis, Luc
Svetchine, Giancarlo Gardin, Marco de Valdivia, Eduard Hueber, Paul
Maurer, John Peck, Jyrki Tasa, Laure Thorel, Hisao Suzuki, Stéphane
Couturier/Archipress, Jean gallus, Sophie de Martino, Joan Mundó,
Hannes, Annemarie Schudel, Miro Zagnoli

Copyright © 1997 Arco Editorial SA
ISBN: 2-88046-296-7

Published and distributed by RotoVision SA
Sheridan House
112-116A Western Road
Hove, East Sussex BN3 1DD
England
Tel. 1273 72 72 68
Fax. 1273 72 72 69

Production and color separation in Singapore by
ProVision Pte. Ltd.
Tel. (65) 334-7720
Fax (65) 334-7721

*Brightly lit spaces*

Light breaks where no sun shines;
Where no sea runs, the waters of the heart
Push in their tides;
And, broken ghosts with glow-worms in their heads,
The things of light
File through the flesh where no flesh decks the bones.

..................................................................................

Light breaks on secret lots,
On tips of thought where thoughts smell in the rain;
When logics die,
The secret of the soil grows through the eye,
And blood jumps in the sun;
Above the waste allotments the dawn halts.

Dylan Thomas

*Light breaks where no sun shines*
*Translation by Esteban Pujals. c. Visor Libros.*

Architecture is not a set of techniques and calculations which convert nature into skyscrapers and sports centers: something in the way of a transforming force capable of emptying a mountain so as to provide the facing for a law court. Architecture is not the science of organizing spaces, nor the study of how to link some activities with others, nor is it the way to think of places which are suitable for work, for free time or for social life. It is not the way to put the countryside into order, nor to connect some places with others, nor to create a favourable atmosphere for meetings, nor to mark out the land and fit it into logical measurements. Neither is it that which permits us to identify buildings, squares or streets, to remember them, to associate them with meanings and even concepts and metaphors; or to simply think of them as nice agreeable places or that they are different to others.

Architecture is not all this, or it is not in the first place. Perhaps this is how it appears, but it is not its origin, or it should not be.

There is a region of architecture which lives at the extremes of thinking, which borders on the memory and the emotions. Here, architecture has to do with light, with the way in which one has knowledge of things, with the brightness of a summer's morning, with sunbeams through the blinds and their hypnotic shadows during a nap on days leisure of, with the intense yellow of bedrooms in winter, lit by a single bulb in a corner, just by the bedside; it has to do with hideaways in the half-shadow of too-wide passages or with the wound of the sun on the shutter of a bedroom window which is dark at two o'clock in the afternoon.

In these extremes of thinking, architecture becomes worn away into

fragments of sensations, personal images which, nevertheless, appear to be surprisingly similar and interchangeable.

Usually, architects tend to explain their buildings through solidly-structured speeches, in which each part is analyzed and each stage studied. They first talk about the way in which the building has to adapt itself to the lot, to integrate itself into the topography, or to respect the urban surroundings. They also explain the volumetric games, the rhetoric of accessing the interior, the ordering of the most complex programs in simple, intelligible spaces, the constructive solutions and technical innovations. In some cases they continue, talking about the way the light penetrates the interior, and even the linking of spaces, of the construction of sequential paths, of the separation between spaces which serve and spaces which are served, or between busy places and

intimate ones. But very few dare to renounce the joint vision of the building, to only evaluate some of the sensations or some of the especially pleasant moments that it might be possible to experience within them. And yet, it is certain that the majority of the people who visit them only retain in their memories these few places.

This book sets out a journey in reverse, which begins with the particular, which mixes completely different buildings, architects with contrary ideas and methods and places that are enormously diverse through that which is the least precise in them.

It does it by passing through all that permits one to perceive the spaces: through the light, through the color, by the textures and materials. It presents different ways of understanding the buildings in relationship with the sun, to the gradation of the light, to its intensity, to the way of introducing it in to interiors.

Paradoxically, the rooms of two houses which have been thought up from theoretical ideas and budgets that are completely opposite, may turn out to be almost identical if they are finished with the same materials and the same color.

The light, the color, the materials, the textures, these make up the face of the spaces, its presence immediate and inescapable.

On the following pages are presented examples of spaces finished with chromatic variations of the primary colors: red, blue and yellow as well as white and grays; or constructed with a predominant material, whether it wood, metal, stone, concrete or brick.

Perhaps it is not an academic vision, but this is not our intention. We do not wish to establish absolute truths, but streams of ideas, seas of impressions, fleeting splendors and intuitions.

Brightly Lit Spaces does not intend to transmit an architectonic discourse, but to provide a direct intuitive relationship with architecture starting with light.

# Brightly lit spaces

# Orientation of light

# Southern light

The apparent rotation of the Sun with respect to the Earth is produced between the two lines of the tropics. For this reason, although the sun always rises in the east and sets in the west, for the countries in the northern hemisphere, the Sun has a southern trajectory and for those of the southern hemisphere, it has a northern trajectory.

This is why light from the south (in the northern hemisphere) always consists of direct sunlight, with greater inclination and less calorific intensity in winter and the opposite in summer.

Southern facing is usually considered to be the best orientation for domestic spaces: the place where the living room and the main rooms of the house are situated. On the other hand, it is not always the most adequate for working because of the reflections on the screens and bright areas on surfaces.

During the cold months, heating costs are much lower than in the rooms facing north and the sensation of comfort is greater.

If the openings are large, it is convenient to have something to protect from the direct summer light: an awning, a porch, a slatted shutter or a slatted blind.

Southern light produces shadows and reflections. It permits one to play with volume, to place elements so that they are outlined against the light, or even if a swimming pool or a small pond is constructed in front of a porch or the windows of the living room, it is possible to produce reflections which are in continuous movement on the walls and ceiling.

Apart from its physical characteristics, there are also a large number of psychological and psychosomatic consequences associated with light. Sunlight produces a feeling of well-being and is healthy. •

On this page, one can see two terraces seen from inside.

Spaces oriented to the south receive sun during almost the whole day and, above all, at midday, the hour when the light and heat are most intense. This is why, in hot countries, it is convenient to protect terraces with awnings, porches or pergolas.

*An aspect of the gallery in a house designed by Dolf Schnebli in Zurich (Switzerland). Perfectly orientated to the south, this space receives sunlight during the whole day.*

# Northern light

Spaces which are orientated to the north do not receive direct light (in the northern hemisphere). It is a diffused light, without shadows or reflections, adequate for working, for painting or for watching television: painters' studios and offices tend to be orientated in this direction. It is also the most adequate for shop windows. It is possible to have large windows open to the north, in order to obtain the maximum possible amount of light without having to fear direct sunlight.

On the other hand it is not very adequate for those rooms where the sensation of comfort is important: bedrooms, dining rooms, living rooms, etc. It can be very interesting, whenever it is possible, to mix northern light with openings in other directions. In this way the space can benefit from the best qualities of both orientations: on one side, the cold, clean, northern light and on the other, the warmth of the direct yellow light (perhaps only a beam of sunlight through a small opening).

In single-family houses it is relatively frequent to site the garage to the north, the stairs, store-rooms or any other room which is not constantly used. However, in very hot countries this orientation is not considered unfavorable during the whole year. On the contrary, in summer, fresh, shady spaces are the more agreeable. The northern slope of the mountains is normally the wettest and where there is more vegetation. This is why it is not strange to find some houses with two living rooms and two patios or gardens: some facing south and the others north.

A person who always finds himself in north-facing rooms, both when working and when at home, who does not often go out for walks, will have very little contact with the sun. This might provoke a feeling of sadness and melancholy, and even bad temper. Yet, nevertheless, this same austerity and coldness may be just right to transmit a ascetic, spiritual feeling.

Northern light does not produce
reflections nor does it dazzle so that
the transparency between the exterior
and the interior is perfect. The slats do
not protect against the sun, rather they
ensure privacy.

Detail of the window over the river, in a
house by Briand & Cardin in Poissy
(France). The window is perfectly
orientated to the north.

Detail of the dining room of a dwelling
designed by Kazuo Shinohara in
Yokohama (Japan). The spaces orientated
to the north do not receive direct sunlight.

Northward orientation allows the
incorporation of picture windows,
here making for a closer
relationship between the living
room and the garden.

# Morning light

On the days when one does not have to get up early to go to work, when it is possible to take one's time with the morning's activities, to slow down the waking up routine, to put the alarm clock to one side and have a slow breakfast, on these days it is possible to appreciate the morning light, through Venetian blinds or in a kitchen flooded with sunlight, like a primitive creating light, life-generating, which is capable of waking up everything, providing them with the energy necessary to recover color, texture and memory.

To achieve this, the orientation has to be linked to the bedrooms, to the kitchen and to the dining room. A person who lives in a group of spaces must be conscious of when he is in each one of them. The effect that light has on the spaces can be substituted for other preferences

only with difficulty. An improved distribution with respect to the rest of the rooms in the house, a larger room, improved acoustic insulation, or even a good view: one may try to improve all this or go to other spaces in the house, but the morning sun loses its meaning in other rooms.

The sun's rays are low, since it is still not very high. Nevertheless, they are not too bothersome. The spaces are still cold and the sun is warm.

However, still more important than the light is the sight of the actual beams. If the openings are sufficiently narrow, or if the light filters through a blind it is possible to make out the profile of the beams, to observe how their shadows shift along the walls of the room. The light itself materializes on the specks of dust hanging, suspended in the air and one can feel the warmth of the rays.

The morning sun's rays are low, but in contrast to the last rays of the evening, they give warmth during the first hours of the day to the spaces which grew cold during the night.

Due to the angle of the sun's rays, the window carpentry is converted into fortuitous pergolas.

On the following page, the architects have placed a metal staircase just in front of the east-facing window so that the morning light is filtered.

It is important to take into account the orientation of a room when choosing the type of finish for the flooring and walls.
On these pages it can be appreciated how the finishes influence the impression transmitted by the illumination of two rooms with the same orientation and at the same time of day.

Evening in Venice (California). A view
from the beach towards a house built
by Antoine Predock.

# Evening light

Daylight begins to lose intensity after a certain
hour of the day. The sun loses itself behind the
roofs of the buildings, but its reflection still
persists in the windows facing east. White walls
shine with greater intensity and with a slightly
yellow tinge, brick walls take on an intense
orange color, all the surfaces in the city are
transformed and the sparkles multiply.

When the sun is sufficiently low, it stops
illuminating the pavements and the asphalt and it
strikes the façades almost perpendicularly. The
city is then converted into a screen.

When it finally disappears, the reverberation
of the light upon the heavenly dome continues to
illuminate the city. The blue of the extreme east
of the horizon grows dark and becomes
impregnated with reflections of rose.

As from this moment and until total darkness
is reached, the light changes constantly, like a
swell on the sea. With the frequency of blinking,
the city undergoes infinitesimal metamorphoses.
And without our hardly noticing it, the outlines of
objects become more diffuse, some objects overlap
others and it is difficult to make out their edges,
all reality draws closer, it becomes camouflaged
within the ever-darkening blue and rose.

The spaces which are orientated to the west
should be protected from the last perpendicular
sunlight and be capable of catching the changes of
light each evening. •

*Evening sun on the west façade of the Turégano house of Alberto Campo Baeza in Pozuelo de Alarcón (Madrid). The panes of glass are levelled in accordance with the walls so that no shadows are produced, only reflections.*

*From the living room window of the house in Glencoe (Illinois), one can watch the nightfall over the snow.*

*On this page there are two views of nightfall on the porch of a house by Geoffrey Pie in Queensland (Australia).*

Steven Haas's house in Long
Island. The windows repeat the
coast's shape.

The enormous twisting windows
permit the observation of the
reflection of the sea on the panes,
mixed with the images of other
interior spaces.

# Overhead light

In an apartment block, unless the dwelling is situated in the attic, the possibility does not often present itself for using overhead light. This type of light is a privilege of single family houses.

The openings can be of many types, of different materials and surfaces: from small, translucent, plastic skylights which can be bought on the market, to more complex structures of metal and glass that can cover complete rooms.

Skylights not only introduce natural light into the interior, they also appraise the rooms in a different way. Low overhead illumination on a wall converts it into an animated element, capable of unfolding different images depending on the direction and intensity of the light rays. The overhead lighting of a staircase gives this architectonic element a symbolic meaning.

The windows and glass partitions imply a more or less explicit relationship between the interior and exterior, while skylights permit a greater isolation from the surroundings and a certain introspection.

In especially noisy and variegated areas this possibility presents itself as a new way to confront the domestic space. It is not strange that in cities such as Tokyo, many single family residences immersed in the urban fabric have been conceived by architects such as Ando, Ito, Naito, Tominaga and Hayakawa, on the basis of interior patios and spaces illuminated with overhead light. It is the way of re-finding silence and tranquillity in an environment that lacks them. •

*John Pawson and Claudio Silvestrin keep the openings in the vertical surfaces to a minimum. There are entrances for low overhead light in almost all the rooms.*

*Taking advantage of natural light does not imply a direct communication between the interior and exterior.*

*An overhead opening at the end of a spiral staircase. Staircases tend to be illuminated from above. In this way one climbs towards the light.*

The subdued light produced by the
overhead light not only increases the
light, but allows the shadows to
express an element of opaque focus.

41

The architect has combined blocks of translucent glass and plates of glass, according to whether he wanted to favor the transparency or only the luminosity.

Two views of the interior patio of the Maison de Science, an apartment block in Suger de Paris Street, designed by Antoine Grumbach.

42

# Gradation
# of light

# Direct light and diffused light

Outside, light varies according to the position and angle of the sun, according to the phases of the moon, on whether the sky is more or less cloudy, depending on the season and on the pollution. When outside we have to adapt ourselves to the light, seeking sunny areas or shady ones.

However, on the inside we have the chance to control the light, to mould it into the form which we wish it to be, in other words we can take it over.

Although we cannot create natural light, we can control its intensity, its direction, its brightness, through perfectly controlled filters, by the design of the openings, by the choice of the surfaces on which the light is reflected: we can transform light through the elements which we are capable of controlling, we can re-create it.

We possess the possibility of reflecting direct light with screens, from sheets of water or walls faced with polished materials, of controlling sunlight with porches, with slatted blinds, with narrow openings through which the light enters in a precise manner, of diffusing it through translucent glass facings or reflecting it on rough surfaces, of introducing light through skylights into spaces orientated to the north or staining the beams by making them bounce against colored walls.

Just as important as the coherent distribution of the spaces, the relationship between some rooms and others, the size of a room relative to the whole, the movements or the relationship with the exterior, just as important as all this, or perhaps more so, is the control of the kind of light that enters each space. •

Several images of the double-
height living room in the house
at 42, Rochester Place in
London, built by David Wild.

The lines of shadows produced on
the walls by the slats mingle with
the structure's dark-gray lacquered
metal profiles.

Depending on where the light comes
from, it will strike in a diffuse
manner (upper left) or directly
(upper right). In this second case, the
slats produce striped shadows
throughout the room.

*Direct illumination through the shutters in the house in Kumamoto (Japan), designed by Antonio Citterio and Terry Dwan.*

Staircase in the house designed by Franco
and Paulo Moro in Tesino (Switzerland).
Two types of light are mixed in the picture:
diffused, which enters through the overhead
skylight on the stairs, and direct, which
comes in through an open door and draws
the shadow outline of a person on the wall.

On the following pages, interior views
of the apartment at 470, Rue du
Dahomey, by Patrick Hardy. Light
arrives via interior patios so that
there is hardly any direct light
anywhere in the house.

*Shutter at the entrance of the house in
Kumamoto by Antonio Citterio and
Terry Dwan.*

# Shadows

Le Corbusier accompanied his famous phrase
"architecture is the play of volumes under the
light" with a picture in which the basic shapes:
the square, the sphere, the cone and the cylinder
appear drawn in clearly differentiated ways, with
illuminated sides and sides in shade and with
their shadows on the floor.

The fact that to demonstrate the importance of
light in architecture, Le Corbusier drew the
objects' shadows with special emphasis, gives us
an idea of this importance on one hand, and shows
that the shadow is not the opposite side to light,
but one of its essential characteristics, that which
gives it a more bodily, a more concrete character.

The Baroque masters of painting, such as
Caravaggio, Rembrandt and Zurbarán, were the
first to realize that there is no better method of
illuminating an object than by surrounding it by
shadow. This same effect which has been applied
to painting can now be transferred to the field of
architecture. The time when light makes itself
more felt, in a church, or through the slats of a
blind, the illumination is only partial, it is a
mixture of light beams and shadows.

Thus, the slits, the narrow openings, the
slatted blinds, the shutters, the pergolas and all
those other elements which filter the light and
throw shadows are, perhaps, the most perfect
way of showing the presence of light in an
evident manner. ●

The living room in the house in Vallvidrera, Barcelona (Spain), by Joan Rodón. The teak wood shutter throws a network of shadows in to the room which changes according to the time of day.

The balcony of the Sag Pond House designed by Agrest & Gandelsonas in Long Island. The small terrace is completely criss-crossed by lines of shadow from the wooden laths.

A pergola in Villa Escarrer in Mallorca (Spain) by Martorell & Bohigas & Mackay. The shadow repeats the same reticulated section of the pergola on the floor.

Casa Villangómez in Ibiza, by Elías Torres and José Antonio Martínez-Lapeña.
The house is situated in a pinewood near the beach. However, its perimeter is completely closed to the exterior, except for narrow openings between the walls. The dwelling itself is organized around an interior patio.

The white walls between the trees act as screens on which the shadows of the pine trees are projected as if they were a shadow pantomime.

On these pages one can observe the
upper floor of the Water/Glass House, a
guest house designed by Kengo Kuma.
There are no opaque walls in this space.
The Japanese architect has worked with
shadows, reflections and transparencies.
For this reason, the elements which he
has used are the slatted canopy, glass
and water.

*The interior of a Bart Prince house.*

# Half-shadows

Dimly lit spaces are becoming ever rarer. Almost everywhere there is a nearby window or a light switch or perhaps a television or computer screen which attracts all of our attention. It is not often that our eyes can lose themselves in the half-shadow, so that our thoughts may escape from precise images.

Half-shadow is an invitation to leave behind any urgent activities and to relate ourselves to the spaces and the people who are around us, in a different manner. The lack of light provokes secrets, incites privacy and silence.

Although in public spaces, in offices, in shops and work-places, half-shadow would not make sense, in fact, in most cases, maximum possible light is sought after: in the private and intimate atmosphere of the domestic space, there is no reason for light to be obligatory when it is not necessary.

Recovering half-shadows means reserving a space for ill-defined activities or even no activity, but for silence and meditation. It is not necessary for it to be a principal space, the living room or the kitchen, not even a bedroom, half-shadows may be left for another, non-defined kind or place: spaces for communication, ante-rooms, lofts, etc., places where children hide and where secrets are born.

One cannot expect a promoter or house salesman to possess the courage to vindicate such a space, it is even unusual for an architect to do so; it has to be a personal decision of the user, the one who is going to live in those spaces, this must be the one to suggest them. ●

In the traditional houses of hot countries, it is usual to encounter cane-covered terraces, since in summer spaces in half-shadow are much more agreeable than those which are excessively sunny.

The interior patio of a house by Tadao Ando.

Dark, damp spaces of the actual terrain are used to an advantage by Agustín Hernández to set up a fresh and exceedingly agreeable space in a Mexican house.

Several pictures of interior
communication spaces which receive
light, thanks to the pavewalls.
Passageways do not necessarily have
to be very well-illuminated, a less
uniform illumination is often much
more attractive.

One of the elements introduced into
architecture during the twentieth
century is the translucent glass block.
This material can be used both as
exterior walls and interior divisions. It
allows the passage of light but not
the image.

# Night

That which allows us to see during the day, causes us to be seen during the night. The reflections of sunlight on the windows prevent us from making out the interiors. Even when the light is diffused and there are no reflections, the interiors are less illuminated and it is difficult to see what is happening within the houses further away than two or three meters. However, when the light decreases and the lamps are lit, the windows are converted into displays. It is difficult to make out the figures in the street, but, on the other hand, we convert ourselves into silent, yet precise images through the windows.

This transparency might mean a certain uncomfortableness, but it can also be attractive, suggestive or even necessary.

In the situation where one wishes to maintain one's privacy, the only solution, which is also the simplest, is to draw the curtains or lower the blinds.

But perhaps it is not uncomfortable that at night the brightly lit living room can be seen from the street, from the beach or the surroundings of an isolated house. After all, to be sitting down on a sofa reading, sewing or chatting is not something shameful or something which should be hidden: it could even be quite moving to see a familiar scene from the street, to recognize one's loved ones, to imagine what they are saying, to watch the scene before entering a few moments later.

For those who have a private garden available, this relationship between the illuminated interior and dark exterior could be the path for developing a different project.

And for those who find themselves in uninhabited surroundings and are waiting for someone, it may even be necessary to keep a light on as a guide, or a candle behind a window. ●

*Nocturnal views of two houses in Westchester (New York) and Malibu (California) by Richard Meier.*

*At night, the bulk of the house is
lost. The image of the house is
made up of the illuminated
interiors: independent scenes seen
through the windows.*

*The entrance of a Jeanne McCallen house in California. Just like a candle behind a window, or a lamp in the forest, the light converts itself into a lure for visitors.*

The illuminated swimming pool of
Luc Svetchine in Nice (France).

The Kidosaki house by Tadao
Ando. At night, there is a greater
intimacy in the exterior than in
the interior. The aspect of the
house changes completely.

A nocturnal view of the Sperl
house in Zerlach (Austria),
constructed by Ernst Gisel Brecht.

# Color

# Blue

Although the association of colors to certain emotions is questionable, it is inevitable to relate them to each of the feelings produced by the objects or elements which we see in these colors. Likewise, there is an inherited chromatic culture, which identifies each color with concepts, ideas and emotions. However, the feelings associated with each one of them may vary according to the cultural environment.

The heavens and the seas are blue. It is a color of wide open spaces and of the depths. Both the heavens and the seas can be gazed at for hours. It is a relaxing color or one associated with relaxing landscapes, but it is also associated with things melancholy, and a certain sadness. It is the color of songs by Billie Holiday and John Lee Hooker.

But it is also the color of the Virgin's robe, of the prince in fairy tales, the Tuaregs and the North American Union army. It is the typical color of jeans (from Genoa fustian), and working overalls, of police uniforms in many countries and of noble blood. In Japanese theatrical productions it is the color of the negative people; in the Kabuki theatre it is the color of evil people and malignant spirits.

In painting, blue did not appear until the end of the Middle Ages, sky blue ousted the golden colors, associated with the divine, used to paint the sky. Dark blue is one of the colors recovered by contemporary art: it is the color of some of the most famous cut-outs of Henri Matisse's old age, of many of the paintings by Joan Miró, of the extraordinary triptych Le Grand Bleu and of the painting *Ceci est la couleur des mes rêves* (the phrase which appears alongside a blue-colored stain) and it is the color of one of the most well-known phases of the work of one of the most relevant artists of the second half of the century, Yves Klein. •

The interior of the Pechauzi house (France) designed by Julie Phipps. The colors vary from yellow to blue, through red; violet, purple, lilac, etc.

Detail of a bedroom painted dark blue, in which a Joan Miró wall carpet has been hung.

A corridor in the Escarrer Villa in
Palma de Mallorca, designed by
Martorell & Bohigas & Mackay.
Some motifs have been painted on
the walls which are reminiscent of
sails or birds, against the blue
background of the sky or the sea, just
as in the paintings by Albert Ràfols-
Casamada.

*Light blue is common in bathrooms and in those rooms where water is used. In this case, the facings have been covered with ceramic gresite.*

*A view of the bedroom in a house in Gaia, by Xavier Sust and Pepita Teixidó. The walls have been painted dark blue.*

The books on the glass coffee table read *LES ORIENTALISTES DE L'ÉCOLE ITALIENNE*.

*The dining room in the le Moult house in Paris, designed by Philippe Starck.*

# Gray

Gray is a synonym for the undefined. Perhaps it is because is it an alternative to the dialectic of opposites, of black and white; or perhaps because it is impossible to achieve a precise image of the color gray, one tends to think more of grays, multiple blended tones.

When a man, a life or a job are said to be gray, it means that they are mediocre and always the same. A gray day is cloudy and overcast.

However, gray can also be the color of spirituality and asceticism. It can be understood as something which is more than a color, as the liberation of color and, even of light, an earlier condition, misty and diffused, closer to the spiritual rather than the actual presence of things.

Gray is the color of Zen, of the gravel gardens of the Kyoto temples.

Gray is common in architecture, it is the color of concrete, of siliceous stone, of lead, of aluminium, of steel, and of chrome plating. It is found not only in the buildings, but also in the streets, in the pavements, in roads, in bridges and in squares.

Concrete facings or metallic surfaces often give rise to reservations when used in the domestic environment as being materials which are too cold or for industrial purposes. However, this attitude is giving way to another form of interpreting these types of materials, that of being elegant and austere at the same time. ●

Two pictures of the Kidosaki house by Tadao Ando. The Japanese architect has renounced color. His architecture makes an in-depth study of the play of shadows and in the study of light. It is an architecture which is associated with silence and the metaphysical. Gray is the essential color of Japanese architecture (as is explained by Henry Plummer in his book Light in Japanese Architecture). Gray removes the meaning from things.

Detail of the staircase in the Kidosaki house.

Several pictures of the house at 84, Portland Road, designed by Stefano de Martino and Alex Wall, former collaborators of OMA (Office for Metropolitan Architecture). Plays of transparencies and compositions with grays, blacks and chrome plating abound.

*The gray of the marble endows the space with great elegance.*

*Two aspects of a house designed by Ada Dewes and Sergio Puentes in San Bernabé (Mexico). An attempt has been made in both the kitchen and bathroom to recover a traditional image.*

The structure's wood has been
varnished in dark gray. The floor is
composed of dark gray ceramic
tiles. The diffused light which enters
the house through the overhead
skylights acquires the gray tones of
the materials.

Two views of the living room in a single-
family house designed by Helmut C.
Schulitz in Lehre (Germany).

91

# Red

Until the end of the last millennium, red was the synonym of colored: coloratus. It is the color with the longest wavelength, it is the first which can be distinguished by the human eye. At a lower frequency is infrared, which can be detected by some animals. At the other extreme is ultraviolet.

Red is also the first color to be perceived by small children, the one that has greatest emotional strength.

It is a color which possesses impact. It is synonymous with danger or warning in almost all of the countries of the world. It is the color used in road signs and in the traffic light stop signs.

It is also the color of blood and hence, of massacres and violence; the color of fire and of heat (the hot water tap is always indicated by the color red).

It can also be a fearful color, that of Hades, of noble birth, of respect, of religion, of the vestments of Buddhist monks or of cardinals and it is also the color of vindication and revolution, the color of communism.

Red is rarely encountered in a pure form in architecture. The red-brown which comes from the earth is more frequent: the color of clay, of bricks, of roof tiles and many traditional stuccos. It continues to be the typical color of rural architecture in many countries, mimetic buildings which are formed from the very earth. This shade of red is completely different, it transmits a feeling of comfort, of protection, of tranquillity

*Detail of the living room. The red
of the wall combines perfectly
with the shades of the parquet.*

*A view of a bedroom in a house
designed by Bascompte and Font in
Barcelona. The facing is finished off in
shades of red.*

*Andrea P. Leers and Jane Weizapfel
combine a salmon color with the wood
and the violet in the interior of a house
in Maine (USA).*

A view of the double spacing of
the staircase. The violet and
the salmon color are both
mixed in different proportions
to the red and blue.

*The architects Dieter and Margret Schmid designed their own home in Biberach (Germany), inspired by Art Nouveau.*

*The admiration that these two architects feel for Antoni Gaudí can be recognized in almost all the spaces.*

Several pictures of houses designed by Mark Mack California: in Sausalito, left and in the Napa Valley, below, the Kirlin Residence and, on the following page, the Knipschild house.

100

*Red is a common color in the
architecture of Mark Mack,
inspired in the haciendas of
Mexico and Texas.*

# Yellow

Yellow is the brightest color. It is the color of the sun and of gold. The more saturated it is, the more intense it is. While the other colors become darker as they are saturated, yellow becomes more brilliant and visible. Perhaps this is the reason why yellow is not very frequent and the ochres are.

The religious painters of the Middle Ages painted the sky and the halos of the saints with gold pigments, as a symbol of divinity. In the Orient, the Sung dynasty adopted yellow as the imperial color and since then it has been a color reserved for the emperor.

Although yellow, associated with gold can be the symbol of prosperity, it can also be identified with infamy and humiliation: the Nazis forced the Jews to wear yellow bracelets on their arms, and the Heretics, in the Spain of the Inquisition, were forced to carry a yellow cross.

Sensationalist newspapers are known as the yellow press and, on the other hand, it is a color which is associated with disease: a yellow flag on a ship means that there is an outbreak of a contagious disease on board.

Yellow is a relatively frequent color in architecture. Ochers are usual in wall facings: paints, stuccos, and even much calcareous stone is of this color.

It is also the color of the light of the majority of incandescent lamps. Yellow light, in contrast to white light is warmer, cosier. ●

Detail of an apartment decorated by
Rita Taskinen in Tampere (Finland).
The walls as well as the floor, the
furniture, the duvet and the lighting,
are the same shade of yellow.

A double height living room in a villa
renovated by Antonio Citterio and
Teresa Ann Dwan in Via Brera in
Milan.

The sun's rays which strike directly on
to yellow surfaces acquire great
intensity.

The Escarrer house in Palma de Mallorca, planned o designed by Martorell & Bohigas & Mackay.

A view of the living room. The room is given shades of yellow by the light shining through the marble screen.

*A view of the double space with
the wooden staircase. Each space
in this house is dominated by a
determined color range.*

The dining room in the Pastor
house in Barcelona, planned and
designed by Alfredo Arribas.

Detail of the dining room in a dwelling
deisgned by Carlos Ferrater on the
Costa Brava.

Various interior views of the house.

# White

White is the color of the clouds, of snow, of milk, of cotton, and of flax, of paper, of candles, of flags of peace, of seagulls, of the Pope, of Christian brides, of mourning in China and in India, it is the color of doctors, tennis players and Snowwhite.

Perhaps white is the most common color in architecture. Lime and plaster are white. In the Mediterranean area, the houses have always been this color, both on the outside and on the inside.

But it is not only the color of popular architecture, it is also that of culture. It is associated with classicism, with the rest of the Roman and Greek cultures, with the marble temples, with the ruins and the statues. Although originally painted, the loss of these pigments due to erosion and time, have transformed the image of classical architecture and converted it into a totally achromatic form of architecture. This is why, today, classicism is associated with white. This is the color of Saint Peter's Basilica in Rome, of Saint Paul's Cathedral in London, the Capitol Building and the White House in Washington. And similarly, it is also the color of temples of other cultures such as the Buddhist Stupas of Kathmandu or the Taj Mahal.

It is also the color of the move towards Modernism, and the International Style: the houses of Le Corbusier, Gropius, Richard Neutra and Adolf Loos are all white. This is associated with the search for simplicity and the approximation to the form.

In the seventies, a group of five North American architects were known as the whites: Richard Meier, Peter Eisemann, John Hedjuk, Michael Graves and Charles Gwathmey.

On this page and the following,
two views of the Harding
Township house, designed by
Richard Meier in New Jersey.

An aspect of the living room of
the Ackerberg house in Malibu, by
Richard Meier.

*The works of Richard Meier are carried out exclusively with materials finished in white. It is a textual architecture, where the volumes and forms articulate under the light.*

*Two details in plaster on the wall in a house on Via Donizetti, Milan by on Franco Raggi.*

*White can also be understood as the absence of color.*

*Empty, white interiors give the impression of more solace. Here, the image corresponds to a house by the Danish architect Wagn Hjorth.*

The living room of the Zorn residence, designed by the Chicago studio of Krueck & Sexton. The architects have used highly-polished materials which produce a multitude of shining reflections.

Artificial lighting is almost always produced in an indirect way. The lights are hidden within the corners and folds of the walls and the false ceiling. This converts the walls into illuminated screens.

# Textures and other materials

# Wood

Until the generalized use of iron in construction, wood was the only material that was capable of being bend and stretched, in other words, it was the only material used to construct non-domed roofs. Moreover, in many regions, especially where there were forests, wood was the material used almost exclusively in architecture, both for the structures themselves and the details and furniture.

There are as many types of wood as there are tree species. They can have widely differing tones, from the very light of the poplar and the birch, to the very dark of the ebony and wengé. In architecture wood is used in many ways: structure, carpentry, enclosure, covering, flooring, furniture, etc. Every type of wood has been adopted for certain uses according to its physical characteristics: fir, pine, oak, birch, purpleheart and cedar for construction, pine, embero and oak for doors, sapele, maple and oak for floorings, beech, walnut, pine and pear for furniture, elm, melis and teak for damp, aggressive environments,

gaboon, palisander, bubinga for decorative wall coverings, padouk, ebony, mahogany for luxury furniture, etc.

According to how the wood is cut, axially, transversely or radially, the surface arrangement of the growth rings will be different; woods which belongs to the coniferous family will not show the typical pores of the leafy woods: there is a complete series of other considerations to take into account, since wood is one of the few materials to come from a living being to be used in architecture.

However, in spite of the variety of types, one can distinguish certain common qualities which separate them from other materials. Without doubt, any kind of wood will provide spaces with an extraordinary warmth and intimacy, a great sensation of comfort. After cutting down the trees and cutting up the trunks and seasoning the planks and cutting the pieces and varnishing the surfaces: after all this treatment, we still see wood as being something natural, friendly and close.

Some images of houses designed by the North American architect Bart Prince. Wood permits a great formal freedom which perfectly adjusts itself to the tendency towards expressionism and lack of moderation of this architect.

Bart Prince's architecture has adopted nature's forms. Some of this houses' elements have been created based on metaphors. In this case we can see how the roof has been constructed from several wooden sunshades.

Two details of the staircase of the
Jyrki Tasa house. Light in Scandinavian
architecture tends to make itself
evident, to concentrate itself into
beams and to cut through the roofs. It
forms part of the Protestant, ascetic
tradition. Wood from the northern
forests is light in color.

Detail of the living room of a house
designed by Françoise-Helene Jourda and
Gilles Perraudin. Wood can be used to
cover floors as well as walls and ceilings.

On the previous pages, some views of
two houses by the Californian architect
Jeanne McCullen. The traditional
architecture of the American Western
houses is made from wooden structures
which, in many cases, remain on view.

On this page, two wooden staircases of
completely different tones.

130

*The terrace of an Antoni de Moragas'
house in Barcelona. The use of wood
has allowed the easy construction of
inlaid floors on an uneven surface so
as to create a completely flat surface.*

*The façade of a house by the
Morphosis group of Los Angeles.*

# Metal

Metal has immediate associations with architecture. It conjures up images of industry and infrastructures. So that, even though it has been a common construction material since the last century, it is still very difficult to relate it to the domestic area. It can be found in specific elements, kitchen utensils, table legs, picture frames, the bathroom taps, lamps, door handles, furniture, etc., but rarely is it the dominant material, the one which decides the atmosphere of the spaces.

However, it is a common material in the building of dwellings, it can be found in the structure, in the piping, in the carpentry and in the roofs. Copper (a metal which oxidizes rapidly and takes on a beautiful green color) and zinc plates often form a part of the exterior image of buildings and shape the urban landscape.

Lately, the hi-tech architecture, although mainly centered on public buildings, has introduced the technological language of glass and metal into some examples of dwellings. Several of the most important architects of this aesthetic trend: Norman Foster, Nicholas Grimshaw, Michael Hopkins, Jourda & Perraudin, etc., have created, from their own architectonic language, a different way of relating domestic spaces with their environment. The light structures and glazed walls try to reduce the buildings' impact on their surroundings. The technology creates a favorable atmosphere for a more exact knowledge of the mechanisms for natural environmental control and its application. Thus, the most technological construction methods end up providing a closer relationship with nature.

An aspect of the living room in a house in Vaise (France), designed by Françoise-Hélène Jourda and Gilles Perraudin.

Two details of the enclosures. The cloth covering creates an air current which softens the sun's rays. The slatted blinds allow the intensity of the light to be controlled.

The block of dwellings, Grand Union Walk, in London, a project by Nicholas Grimshaw, presents an industrial aspect due to the use of metallic plate finishes.

An aspect of the living room with views of the Grand Union Canal. The interior is illuminated through large double height skylights.

*Detail of the roof of a dwelling
by Gabriel Poole by Lake Weyba
in Queensland (Australia).*

*An aspect of the living room.*
*The metallic materials are*
*capable of transmitting an*
*impression of greater lightness.*

# Brick

Brick construction is one of the oldest techniques. It has been one of the most utilized materials during centuries and it still is today. They are made from baked clay, that means from the Earth, from that which is closest to us. They are easy to manufacture, easy to use and they are cheap. They are used throughout almost the entire whole world.

Bricks can be used as a structural material. Buildings which have brick load-bearing walls, even though they may not be built too high, are not exposed to the dangers of oxidation which is afflicts steel and reinforced concrete structures.

Bricks may have very different qualities depending on the type of clay, the manufacturing method and the baking temperature and mould. These are essential qualities for the final aspect of the walls. On the other hand, it is linked to techniques and a tradition which, in a constructive sense may stand in the way, it would be wise to respect it so that the appearance is not false or deceptive. According to the quality of the material and the technique used, the aspect may vary from the great monumental Roman works or the imperial Chinese palaces to the ancient seaport warehouses.

In the interiors, as opposed to the capacity of the faced surfaces to remove space, bricks introduce the materiality, that which is original and little-worked. Bricks absorb light. Sunlight converts them into warm, throbbing elements.

The North American Architect, Louis Kahn states that the sun is never so beautiful as when it is reflected on a brick wall. •

On page 142. A view of the glass gallery of a dwelling constructed by Sainz de Oíza on the outskirts of Madrid. The general aesthetics of the dwelling try to recover the image of Roman architecture.

On the previous page, a view of the double space of the staircase of a house by Artigas and Sanabria in Barcelona.

On these pages, various views of the Donadio house by Gabriella Ioli Carmassi. The brick wall structure gives the house a classic appearance. The interior and exterior present identical finishes: on-view brick and ceramic tiles. The great staircase in the hall emphasizes the continuity between the two spaces.

144

An interior view of the Bom Jesus House
of the portuguese architect Eduardo
Souto de Moura.

# Stone

There are two main types of stone found in construction: the siliceous type in shades of gray, and the calcareous type found in ochres and browns. Both can be found with two different finishes: on the one hand, taken from the quarry or simply collected to construct rough stone walls, this means with their original appearance, a rough and irregular surface, and on the other, in polished rectangular pieces, used as a facing as in a pavement or in cladding.

In interiors, the visual effect of the two treatments is completely different, almost opposite. The polished stone: marble, granite, travertine, onyx, etc., smooth and brilliant, with veins and encrusted with other materials, are associated with luxury, with sumptuous and palatial environments. Walls covered with stone are perfect, immaculate facings, like enormous jewels. However, they create a cold and distant atmosphere. Normally, interior stone-faced walls are combined with other kinds of materials: wood, or painted plaster surfaces. On the other hand, they tend to be thought of as unitary, compact elements, in which it is difficult to make apertures.

In contrast, when the stone is simply cut and left unpolished, the character of the rooms is completely different. The rough surfaces blur the light, the irregularities produce shadows and the joins acquire a greater presence. The walls transmit a simple, primitive image of heavy, austere construction which appears to belong to another age. Within recent Portuguese architecture, the work of Souto de Moura and Joao Alvaro Rocha has developed better than anyone this contrast between the rough and the smooth, between modern geometrical perfection and the forcefulness of nature. ●

A country house in Mesao Frio in Portugal. It was designed by the architect Joao Alvaro Rocha.

The contrast of the rough texture of the stone with the pure white forms of the walls is a resource used by other present-day Portuguese architects, such as Eduardo Souto de Moura or Alvaro Siza.

Several views of a house designed by John Keenen and Terence Riley in New Jersey (USA). The architects combine the solidity of the stone on the ground floor with the lightness of the glass and metal on the first floor.

In interiors, John Keenen and Terence Riley use stone with two different kinds of finish. While the walls are of rough stone, the flooring is of polished, cut stone.

# Concrete

The use of concrete in the domestic space continues to be rather infrequent. Even though it may be the most commonly-used material in the construction of building structures, it is rarely to be seen in the interiors of houses.

It is not an expensive material. Concrete flooring can work out much cheaper than one of stone, tile or wood. However, it is a material whose appearance can vary enormously with the chosen components and finishes.

In fact, concrete is more a family of materials, rather than just a single material. Although, in its most well-known form, it is a gray color, there is no reason why it always has to be that way. It can possess other color tones depending on the type of aggregate (the granular material used together

with cement to make the concrete) used and the introduction of pigments and other additives.

In the same way, its texture may be rough or extremely smooth. The type of formwork, the aggregate size, and a greater or lesser vibration while the concrete is still fresh, will decide the type of surface. The finer and more regular the formwork, a metallic one, for example, the smaller the aggregate and a greater vibration, will produce a smoother surface.

All this demonstrates that it is a mistake to identify this material with the normal, untidy appearance of the concrete used in large structures. It is possible to obtain elegant finishes, which, at the same time are both simple and sober, and surfaces as brilliant as polished stone.

*One of the characteristic elements of concrete are the formwork joints and shrinkage, which have an inevitable effect on the final appearance of the building.*

On these pages various aspects of the
Kidosaki, Tadao Ando house can be
seen. This architect has popularized a
construction technique and aesthetic in
Japan, associated with the smooth
surfaces and pure forms of concrete.

*The gray tones of concrete cause one's attention to shift from the actual shapes to the phenomena being experienced.*

*Below, two views of a house designed by Agustín Hernández in Mexico.*

*Concrete permits great technical displays, thanks to its structural character.*

Two images of the Cube House by Mioyuki Shirakawa. By using the same materials and techniques, architecture in widely-separated places can achieve similar appearances.

When concrete is less polished, it has an industrial appearance which can be developed to create thought-provoking images.